SHADOWS

Poems of Reflection and Life

Michelle Sarasin

TABLE OF CONTENTS

Part 3: Ghosts of the Past

Part 4: A Story Without An End

Part 5: The Author's Reflection

SHADOWS

Prelude

I wrote *Shadows* nearly 12 years from the start of suffering from depression. Through this time, I've experienced anxiety, domestic violence, emotional abuse, true love, loss, and grief over dreams, loved ones, and my own life. Today, as I write this prelude, I am in some ways both stronger and weaker than I was 12 years ago. I was a child when my life truly started and now I am an adult and realize the old cliché that, so many have said, rings true; *for it is not the years lived, it is the life lived in the years.*
I have lived more years than my age would have you believe. I have gained the wisdom, the knowledge, and the love to know that life; no matter the way, will always be bigger than me. *Shadows* is a book of reflection of my life thus far. I know that there are those out there whether older or a bit younger, that may be able to connect on a deeper level to each poem. I wrote this collection of poetry after years of trial and tribulation and I hope that as you read each poem, you will feel your own "years within" come to life and inspire you to walk on – stronger than before.
To conclude, *Shadows* is a poetry collection that serves to reveal a part of my soul that I know too well, the "dark haven." It is this darkness that I never want to forget because one day, should I ever find happiness in this life, I will never forget

how I found it – should I ever need to find it again.
This book of poems is the reflection of strength, truth, darkness, struggle, and most importantly – love. All of which I have *too* much experience with.
I am sharing my life with you, fellow survivor, in the hopes that you hear my soul and realize that whatever you are going through, you will never be alone (at least, not with this *shadow* nearby).

Enjoy!
Michelle Sarasin

Part I
Shadows of the Soul

Soul in the Shadows

My soul is in the shadows,
On the inside looking out,
The window within my eyes,
Is fogged with the tears, years shed.

In denial of all that I am,
Life has been lived,
And yet it has not begun.
I wonder when the day will come,
When I will see and love the sun.

For the first time I am faced,
With a part of my heart missing,
My soul is complete because I have loved,
And I have lost.

Still I am scared to face the truth.
Home is so far away as I stay unable,
To clear my soul from the shadows.

In this dark state of reality's honesty,
My soul stays hidden,
This is my soul in the shadows...

Into the Deep

Deep within the confines of life,
Lies the dreams of the many,
Fallen and broken.

Happiness is just a word,
Feeling is an all-encompassing emotion,
Life is a state of mind – as we so choose.

Hasn't matter the day,
Society claims to us always,
That one life fits all.

And we rely on this notion,
Because it is too hard to think.
This life they have claimed,

Is the crutch that helps us stand tall.
Yet I feel so small when I think,
Of all they made me try to be.

Now I am confused,
Now I am saddened,
By the life left behind me.

The possibility that I was afraid,
Scares me the most,
For I feel as though at times,

I missed out because I chose,
To stand in oblivion,
I hate to admit, but it was a rebellion.

Rebellion is strange,
We think we go against the tide,
When really all we're doing,

Is wasting our time.
Think about why we rebel,
Against authority's firm hand,

Then you realize,
The line drawn in the deepness of the sand.
'Cause if what we really want,

Lies within giving up this fight,
Then the fight just to be against,
Is nothing more than a child unrepentance.

Into the deep belonging,
Of the dreams that keep me alive.
For if I ever give up,

Then there is nothing more to strive.
For if life loses the will to wonder,
The will to walk the path of fear,

Then we lose our purpose of self-worth,
We lose everything we wanted to feel.
So, please, if life is of any worth to you,

Take time to go against the rebellion,
And do what you want,
Not because they don't want it,

But because it makes you feel,
The word that can be so much more,
Than just a word;

Happiness.
Into the deep dark depths of dreams,
Where tragedy, heartbreak,

And emptiness lies,
Yet you realize how brave you were,
To walk against the tide.

Not because they encouraged it,
But because it was the right thing for you.
For every path not taken,

Is a dream that will never come true.
Down the road when you get to wherever,
You might just realize something strange,

Something that goes against,
Everything they say –
That dreams are not for the faint at heart,

But rather for the brave.
Because darkness has but one enemy –
The truth and when we seek that truth,

We understand that happiness,
Which truly means self-realization,
Keeps us alive.

I can't say that I have lived,
The life destiny had fated.
But I have yet to let go,

Of something so much bigger –
My dreams, for within me lies,
A heart that is stronger,

Than my willingness to forsake.
All that I have ever known,
All that I have ever done,

All the things I forgot to learn,
Are buried in the depths of the past.
But if one thing is ever certain,

I know that my dreams,
Though they may stay just dreams,
Will forever last.

Because I never let go,
I never see more,
Than the dreams I've been given,

I never let myself believe,
That there is a limit.
For dreams are like flowers,

They blossom, and they can die,
Yet they can grow along with our hearts,
They can see the light in the dark.

So even when the light fades,
And the shadows around me call,
I know that this fire still burns,

Deeply within my soul.
I promise this faithful dream,
That I will never let go.

This dream has seen me through,
I will never let it go.
Whatever may happen,

Wherever my life may tread,
I will never let go of this dream,
For my love lies within its soul.

How Many Times

How many times have I hurt you,
To deserve the punishments, you bring?
How many times do I have to lie in my grave,
Until you even up the score?
How many sins have I done against you,
How many wrongs will you have to right on my
heart?

How many times do you have to wound me,
Until the war within yourself is over?
And how many times will people say it's not my
fault,
Until they see that the devil still has his chains
around my heart?

How many times will I make the same mistake,
Until I know how to walk away?
How many times will you hurt me,
Until you get tired of fighting a one-sided war?

How many times and how many scars do you
need to slash on my heart,
Until you finally say goodbye...

Worlds Collide

Worlds collide like thunder and lighting.
We are star-crossed,
And fated to an attraction;

So fatal to our societal status,
That life takes on,
A whole new meaning.

Worlds collide like black and white.
We realized the moment our eyes met,
That our lives were forever altered.

Worlds collide like day and night.
We have crossed paths,
Whether it is destiny's fate,

Or something we've created,
Within our hearts,
We are in love and there's no turning back.

Let worlds collide,
Let them grow in time,
Let them talk about yours and mine.

For if I have you then life is more,
Than anything they can serve to us.
For across the room I already know,

This dress I am wearing,
And the suit you are bearing,
Mean that the dance has just begun.

Shadows – Michelle Sarasin

So, you come over and take my hand,
Prince and princess and we dance,
To the worlds indifferent,

Lives we never thought we'd know.
Yet I know I love you,
And if these worlds are to stay parted,

In this life and in this moment,
Than we shall be reunited in glory,
And they will bow for mercy,

For one has no right to condemn love.
This is our time and our dance,
You are unafraid to take my hand,

Even though worlds collide.
Our worlds collide...
Like a spectral of shadows,

Colors of sentiments,
Gather 'round as we dance.
So, let the shadows whisper,

For that is all they can do.
They can't have us if we don't let them,
They can't make us into their effigy,

They can't stop love from falling.
Worlds collide like we have tonight;
In our worlds this love will never be right.

But love sees nothing but you and I,
So, let our worlds collide...
Let the day turn into night,

We are a rare phenomenon.
Love is as strong as we make it.
As boundless as we choose it to be,

No matter what they say,
Our worlds collide like crashing waves,
Our time runs faster,

With each twirl of the hand,
Our love is nothing,
But destiny between you and me.

Worlds collide...
Love,
An epic tale of beauty.

Edge of Darkness

Resting on the edge of darkness,
My feet dangling off the pier,
As I sit here with my palms,
Faced down feeling the wood,
Splint into flesh as if it can't get enough,
I look out onto the bleak horizon.

I am lonely and off the beaten path,
I am lifeless in the eyes,
Of this bitter darkness.

The sky is gray and white and foggy,
My eyes are a replacement for the mist.
Hidden, I am, by the shadows,
Far off in the distance,
Unto the edges of the fearsome waters.

The tide came in,
The day the world struck me,
As though I was a tree,
And it was the force of nature,
Lightning piercing my edges,
Until I fell to ashes,
Now I am lost and torn apart,
You may find me in the wind.

But you won't,
Because the shadows,
In this forlorn sky,
Hide the edge in which I now stand on,
So you will never see the truth within.

For the curtains are closed,
As you seek the finale,
Pushing me to find my way,
Off the edge of darkness.

My broken heart,
Dispersed all around,
Has touched each edge,
Now I am bound.

One piece has fallen off,
Into the angry waters of the rain,

Then another,
Then the last one,
And now...

Shadows

Shadows among shadows,
Stars among moon glow,
The graying of the dawning sky,
Reflection of the days gone by.

When life trails my dreams,
Though I am ready to make first tracks,
I can't help by feel my shadow,
Calling me back to the past.

So shadows like skeletons,
Hanging in my closet like knitted coats,
Haunt me in my dawning days,
Until I no longer fear the shadows of my past's
holy ghosts.

Heart of the Night

The backdrop of the full moon,
Water crashing along solitary shores,
Footsteps play in the water,
As I dance among the stars.

Music of the ocean,
Audience of the sea creatures –
Mermaids and trawls,
Life of a night so free
I can feel love touching me....

Baring down like an invisible rain,
As I play in heart of the night!

Left and Right

I go right, you go left,
When I went left,
You took a while,
But when right.

Then I went right,
Back to where I started from –
The day you decided,
You wanted to be left alone.

So part of me is gone,
Broken and torn,
Shattered, my heart worn,
Strength, to the left – newfound strength,
Strength to move on.

Then there is the right of me,
Telling me it isn't over,
Ne'er it will ever be,
Still what's left in it for me?

Love is true in my heart,
Lies are the love beheld in yours,
Like green grasses under thick snow,
I stayed for the winter,
In the spring you let me go.

So I ask this to the face I knew,
And the soul whose eyes burn through –

My side of this love's innocence,
Yet I can't help but shy away,
From love shunned.

Now I must face this world,
Without you,
I am alone.

Shadows of the Mist

Toes curled on the edges of the dock,
I close my eyes and breathe.

The waves of the sea,
And the salt of my tears,

Reflect within –
the shadows of the mist.

Time stands still as the fog lingers,
The wind from Satan's hand,

Tightening the edges of my bare feet,
The dress I wear is a shade of light,

Yet still the light emanating from thyself,
Stares into the nothingness of life's desire.

While reflecting within –
the shadows of the mist.

My life hangs in the balance,
My heart is felt within my breast softly in my
heavy hand.

The tide rages among the wood,
My skin feels the cold of God's loving nature.

Here I stand with invisible wings yonder –
the shadows of the mist.

Hostages

Like infants, they cry out,
But they speak not a sensible word.
They watch and see,
More than they ever should,
Their innocence lost by the view.

To the one they follow,
All hope is lost,
Droning out the sound,
Of their mother's mouth.

Who knows why they do any of it?
If they stopped and refused,
Would there be no more war?

Hostages,
Slaves at the hand off the Devil's sword,
Followers, prisoners,
Strangers to the cause,
Chained up inside hallow walls,
The hostages' cries are the choir,
Ignored by the sleeping knight.

Like an arranged marriage,
They toss and turn,
Desperately trying to avoid,
The flames that spread,
Blood and tears, self-destruction shed.
Their voices echo,
Beneath the surface of the earth;
Volcanic eruption seized by evil's berth.

Dark Haven

In the rapture of my dark haven,
I imagine I am over the rainbow.

I imagine a time of life and love;
I close my eyes tightly,
Hoping to imagine this time into reality.

In a corner with the lights off,
Darkness surrounding me,
Like shadows unseen,
I close my eyes and I dream of a life,
I believe was meant for me.

My head is tucked into my arms,
My knees bent,
A resting place for my elbows,
My jeans a towel for my tears.
I am curled up in the confines of my mind,
Lost, alone, afraid of the false light.

The Devil is always hard to see,
Even when he or she is right before me.
Within this dark haven, though,
He can't see me, no he can't see me.

Because I am a refusal to the storm outside.

In this dark haven, I am safe and nullified,
To the things that made me soak my jeans,
And the people who made me feel so weak,
And the dreams broken, shattered before me.

Shadows – Michelle Sarasin

I am uncontrollably,
Looking on the outside into me.

My dark haven lies,
In every dream unsatisfied,
And every wish never to come true,
And every prayer I longed,
To have been unanswered.

I don't hear the angels sing,
I don't see love,
Dancing about the kitchen floor,
I don't even see the worthiness,
In my dreams,
Forsaken God has left me.

I am caught up in,
The spiral of shadows,
The rapture of the past,
The dark haven of my very being.

Like a black cat traveling in the night,
You will never see the love inside,
Until I look up with dry,
Fearless, courageous eyes.

Still my dark haven,
Ever remains, the safest place –
I could ever dream.

Mystified Beauty

Step into a dream world,
A place you've never been,
One of dark mystified beauty,
The call of Heaven sent.

Hear this call,
Wild and passion never ending.
Journey to the outer limits of your soul –
For if ever the soul stops yearning,
For anything but love, then life is dormant.

Dark, mystified, passionate and untamed,
Long for everything, stop at nothing,
Until your soul holds the secret;
The lesson of beautiful life learned,
The struggles that led,
To this beautiful life earned.

Life is fickle and hardly ever free,
In the pangs of this ailing society.
Yet I know they could never take my spirit –
For they could never read its scroll.

And if ever I should find myself,
Lost in their dark cold,
I will have a way back home.
For the dark mystified beauty within,
There is a light that calls only myself.

It is my soul, it is my love,
It is my only hope.
I am dark, mystified and,
Boundless to circumstance,

I hold all the world's tortures,
Within thy heart,
Until I find a way to heal them.
I am calling out –
Through the opposing silence,
There is an echo that just won't die away.

This dark mystified beauty;
For me there will come a day.
I will hear my precious refrain,
Calling back to me,
Calling back to my dark mystified self –
The one you could never know,

Calling me back home.

Shadows of the Soul

Shadows surround,
The very being of my soul.

I am lost. I am alone.
I am widowed from the light.

Yet I stand and walk with grace,
And I will come face to face with –
Each and every demon,
Each and every star,
Each and every time they told me,
I'd never it make this far.

So, shadows coming from years far and near,
Surround the very being of my soul.

I am not far from the light –
Still I can quite reach,
Because I can't see through,
The illusion of these shadows.

Though hope is a friend,
That tends to this despair within;
I still see no escape,
From the darkness of the shadows.

But I feel a warmth within my spirit,
One they can never take away.
Shadows dancing around me,
Like fairies you cannot see,

But I believe because I know,
Miracles are few and far between,
And the only miracle,
That could ever mean anything to me –
Would be the miracle of,
Healing this longing to break free...

From the shadows, one day, I will emerge.

PART 2
BECKONING CALL

Beckoning Call

Love's beckoning call,
Strikes through my heart,
Like lighting to a tree,
Or water to a fire.

I hear it in my dreams,
I see it in the eyes of the moon,
I swear by it when you ask me,
I give it faith when Heaven loses hope.

Yet I can't feel it, always,
Ever lonely through my days and nights.
I try to follow it, yet like a child,
It hides on me, teases me, tortures me.

So, I call to Love's beckoning,
I sing the song it asks of me.
My voice sings the melody,
Life's torrent wind plays the harmony.

Still I don't know where,
I can't look to see,
Love's beckoning call,
Oh, how with such desire – it calls out to me!

Illusion Drifter

Drifting into an illusion,
The shadows call me forth.
The blinding fog impales me,
The spiral of darkness rolls on.

This yearning to live,
Another place and time,
Another way, another life,
Another world entire.

This desire encompasses me,
The shadows create something I can't reach,
Though my heart feels it there with me,
I wonder –
Where will these shadows take me?

Crossroads

Today as I write this,
I am at the crossroads of my life.
I see the dark and I see the road,
That I believe will lead me,
Towards the light.

I have no idea where this narrow road,
Which is long and barely taken,
Will end up and if I should finish,
I wonder – will it be then I discover,

That I made the right choice,
To stay on this path, beaten at every step –
With the sins and the secrets, I have kept.
Within my soul lies,
The key to a great and beautiful life.

But I can't find the key to open,
I can't find the torch,
To dim the darkness inside,
So, I stand here at the crossroads –
Of life and of dreams.

I stay still and look with wonder,
Where each path will lead me.
I travel down the road where dreams,
Either meet a bitter or sweet end.

There is no middle to the crossroads,
My life continues to descend,
I can't see the road ahead of me,

But I regret to know what's coming.

If somehow, I can change my foolish ways,
If somehow, I can turn the day ahead;
Into something my spirit can feed off of,
Lead me out of this darkness,
Inside my mind,

Change this misery,
Into something, so strong,
My remorseful heart, cannot deny.
Yet in the shadows if I see,
Reflections of the path still ahead of me,

I will wonder and I will lose faith,
I will change, and I will try again,
And I will see the sun,
I will reach the top of the mountain.

My choice of walking,
Down the narrow path,
At the crossroads I stand before,
Love will lead me, someday,
To Heaven's door.

No More Rain

I woke up this morning,
In a dream-like state,
Able to make my way to the point,
Of knowing my reality.
I saw my reflection in a dirty old window,
My eyes looked sad, my face worn out.

I don't remember anything after that,
Except for one thing,
I realized was the truth;
All my heart's desire is to have no more rain.

I feel like I don't know where to go,
What to do, where to turn.
Like a sun hiding behind the clouds,
I am forced to wait,
Until they move themselves.

Patience is a virtue,
I know not how long it will last,
But God-willing it won't break me,
Until the final piece,
Of the puzzle of my heart is washed away,
By the seemingly endless rain.

So I sit here and wait until,
The Lord shines his star on me,
To tell me that he will walk,
Through the good times,
As he has the bad, with me,
Until I make it home.

Like a rabbit I sleep in the beauty,
Of lifetime's air,
Never knowing my divine purpose,
Yet always on edge in case the clearing rain,
Brings on a rainbow,
And I can again leap freely.

No more rain,
Give me a chance,
To wash away my own tears.

No more rain,
I am ready to see the sunlight.

Please, God, no more rain,
Let me know that Heaven,
Is not too far away.

No more rain.

Shadows of Despair

Hoarding up around me –
Are these shadows of despair.
To my left and to my right –
Behind me, facing me, beside me.
I hold onto to this feeling –
Because I know it best,
And it knows me –
I am its shadow in distress.

Life isn't meant for the faint of heart,
It was meant for the ones who choose,
To never ever give up.
So, though I give into,
The smoky shadows of despair,

Though I wish,
These shadows were empty,
Like a crystal glass,
Once filled with the sweet quench,
I can't help but hold onto every shadow,
To which my tears filled with their despair.

To know is to feel and to feel is to love,
These shadows of despair –
Are shadows raining from Heaven above;
I will never forget which shadows,
I have risen from.

Without Warning

Without warning you called her forth,
Her spirit lifted as it reigned down her last
goodbye.

Within me, my mother's intuition,
Called out to me – though like the yawning of her
sweet pink lips,
I could only sing back without knowing the
meaning of this perceived warning.

Unexpected and undeserved,
You took her away from me,
As though she was never my precious baby.
The why is still unknown,
The how is even greater –
Yet always I think of when,
Heaven's perfection guided my love home again.

Without warning you took her,
You took her away from me,
But I know that there will never be,
Enough time I will have to spend with thee.

Though I miss her so longingly,
In my heart I hold her like I had just a few
precious times before.
I know one day I will be reunited with her –
In the shadows of Heaven,
We'll stay forever more.

I miss you, my Majesty.

Dawn of the Night

The dawn of the night is upon me,
Quietly I sleep without fear,
I hear the call of the wilderness,
In this place that encompasses,
The very depth of my darkness.

I seek the dawn of a new day,
Somewhere far off in my dreams,
While the earth around me silently waits,
For heaven to conquer the devil's nightmare.

Wolves under the borealis,
Capture the essence of heaven on earth,
The wonderment of being a spirit,
The cold reality of being a human all alone.

So, I hear aurora's call,
I hold no promises to her northern sky,
Yet I keep within me her secret,
Ponder her heavenly cry.

Time is the ultimate keeper of life,
Fate is the ultimate journey to the end,
I am the slave to the ultimate master,
Love has become the enemy to my dark state.

Still, I cry out for the dawn of the night.

Shadows of Hope

Shadows of hope,
Cross the window,
Where the sun used to be.

They take my tears,
And draw my face on the glass,
As if they are mocking me.

But I keep thinking,
If I try a little harder,
To look through these shadows,

Then somehow,
I will see these shadows replaced with light,
Where the fog will one day – *used* to be.

Child's Heart

I don't care much for the sun,
I am a nighttime type of gal,
I have no use for the clouds,
When I could reach for the stars.

Every night as I pray,
I look out into the heavens,
And I talk to the moon,
Wishing I could be just like the night sky,
Letting the darkness be.

My fears will wash away,
As I turn to admire you,
The moon will give me all the light I need,
To make it through,
This life and the next will forever be –
My destiny...

I want to be as bright as the moon,
Shine like the stars,
And fill the world,
With peace from the heavens.

Darkness has no place in a child's heart.

As I go through the daytime,
I yearn for the night –
Wishing that the calmness,
Of the nighttime breeze,
Would sing to me as it brushes my face.

I know it's talking to me,
The man in the moon is listening,
And watching me.

I wish on a star and it becomes a prayer,
As my loneliness turns into a longing love,
Traveling far to be wherever you are.

As I lay me down to sleep,
I pray for all the stars to keep,
Shining their way into my heart,
The moon being my guardian angel,
Lightness of love never ever stops.

The heavens are still,
And watch over this girl –
Who never seems to fit right,
With the sun and its pearls.

But I can touch the stars, kiss the moon,
And hear the angels sing,
Their sweet lullaby from the heavens.
And I can dream of a time and a place,
Where the night light never goes out.

Darkness has no place in a child's heart,
Darkness has no place in a child's heart.

Darkness has no place in *this* child's heart.

Call of the Bottle

Ever heard the call of the bottle –
Shaking beneath your trembling fingers,
Calling you to another place,
Where destruction, bittersweet denial,
And the death of love await?

Ever heard the call of the bottle –
Ringing in your ears,
Like a song stuck in your head?
There is nothing you can do,
Nothing you can say,
Nothing you can do to keep 'em away,
From the call of the bottle.

Ever heard the call of the bottle –
Lying to you like a cheating lover?
Fire burning into your flesh,
Barely reaching your heart.

Problems, like shadows, surround you,
So, you stay in the dark with the bottle,
You heard call out to you,
Like an angel from Hell,
Thinking that you are not strong enough,
To conquer this, overwhelm.

Yet you know that all your problems,
No matter how near or far,
Will still be there tomorrow,
When you wake up – wherever you are.

Ever heard the call of the bottle –
When you are lonely among friends?
Just want to have fun –
This pageant of pleasantry never ends.

So, you think just one more shot,
Won't kill you,
Because you've taken so many,
That anything after this,
Will flow through you,
Anything that you can tell yourself,
It won't stop you from having one more.

Ever heard this seething call of the bottle?
Like a banshee it calls you to your death,
But in between sweet denial,
And learned bitterness,
This call is an escape and relief,
From your hope's merciless.

Life, though, is about so much more,
There is a beginning,
So merciless and cold,
There is an end,
When it comes, only God knows.

But the bottle falls somewhere in the middle.
You fall for this illusion like you did,
Your unfaithful lover – the eyes say it all,
When they say nothing...

Love, like a ship in a bottle,
The mirage of the fall.

Ever heard the call of the bottle –
When you silently watch,
The mud slide down?
There is nothing you can do to stop it,
In its misery your innocent soul drowns.

Escape is a word only cowards know,
So, you stay and suffer,
While their eyes gloss over,
And you pray that mercy shows – please!
Reveal a way to silence the call of the bottle.

Love's Jeopardy

Love is the heart's jeopardy,
Risk all and may gain nothing,
Gamble nothing and may lose all.

Don't tell me how my heart feels,
Leave me to the love within,
I live here and I will die here.

Love is the dream,
The dream where nightmares,
Are barred and turned away.

Love is a gift,
From the heavens and the gods,
A gift bigger than the purpose of one.

Love is the desire,
In which all succumbs,
Even the devil within.

Yet everything and everyone,
Our love overcomes,
Jeopardizes are hearts.

For where tears break through,
Eyes see into a soul for the first time,
So alive is the spirit in which our love rests,

We are left with nothing,
Unless we love until we have nothing left.
For love's jeopardy,
Is worth my every breath.

PART 3
GHOSTS OF THE PAST

Ghosts of the Past

The haunting souls of the past,
Are the scariest ones to ignore.
Because they know what you've done,
Mistakes made from before.
The ghosts hold a pillar of regrets,
And they block the clear mind way.

Ghosts of the past,
Hold fears, tears, and life.
I can only remember the misery,
But I can't let them get what they want,
Not going to take my life away.

Their eyes are pure black,
And I can put my hand through their bodies,
Because they are not really here anymore –
Or are they?
They say it's all in my mind,
But I cannot hide the hurt,
I carry within them, by my side.

I wish I *could* let go of the ghosts of the past,
But they follow me, I am their leader.
If I jump off a balcony,
Would they go with me?
Or would they be staring down at me –
Saying their goodbyes...

When I Think of Love

I always think of you,
When I think of love.

You are always a figure,
In this illusion we once thought possible.

I'm afraid to love anybody else,
I know they could never be you.

Still I wonder what would happen,
If you came back and told me the truth.

I always think of you,
When I think of love.

I miss the times you wondered,
If I'd still be here,

Waiting for you as I still am,
Though I know the line is as thin as the thread,

The needle is as sharp because,
It never touched the crimson of this sheet,

Covering up our bodies,
The anger raging under this numbing heat.

I need to know if you cared,
For love is now an afterthought,

Tangled in the web your made,
The lies failed to illuminate,

The very thickness of this,
Which you've given the name of love to,

Yet when I think of this feeling,
I always think of you.

When I think of love,
I still always think of you.

When I think of love,
I always think of you.

When I think of love,
I always think of *you*.

Illusion of the Shadows

Bring me naïve peace,
Illusion of the shadows.

Dance upon the wall,
While I fall into this metaphorical hole;
My beautiful illusion of reality captivated
In the illusion of the shadows.

Masked is the girl they thought they knew,
Driven by the love which still holds true,
Dancing shadows in the veil of the humid night.

Take me through the portal,
Where the blinding mists reveal your secret,
To this magical illusion of the light.

Illusion of the shadows swirl me around,
As though my heart were pieces of debris in a
tornado,

Carry me over the rainbow,
For a moment I am sober,
From the darkness that befell me.

So I touch the illusion of the shadows,
Within my sleeping heart,
And I carry the puppet 's mask,
You'll never know me –
Unless you dare enter through the mists.

Illusion of the shadows – in this life,
I am bound to your bittersweet kiss.

Illuminating illusion dancing with me,
To the tune of life's sweet misery,
Swept away in the illusion of the shadows.

Hearing thy blessed lost souls sing,
Hearing the chants of love,
Rise through the mystery above,
Grasping my spirit at its strongest –
Is the hallowed illusion of the shadows.

Within your soul I dance,
To the song written for thy own,
Illusion of the shadows.

Shadows of Dreams

I can see the future in my dreams,
The present I can see when I awaken,
My past shadows me as I walk along,

Shadows of dreams,
Both broken and new,
Lead me back to this yearning,

Of knowing if ever I am,
To be okay,
Dreams must shadow me every which way.

Journeys come and go,
But memories stay strong enough,
To haunt me until I face my brink.

I need to know if there is a God,
I need to know if He is with me,
I need to know if life is worth living.

In your eyes, I see my life –
The reason, the only one,
I need to continue breathing.

Though everything has gone,
You have given me enough strength,
To carry on –

One more day;
My life has not claimed,
The death of me.

Above all this darkness,
Under all the bleak,
Between all the chaos,

I see you.
You are the shadow,
Of my dreams.

Swept Away

Swept away,
In the ho-hum thoughts of the day,
I think to myself what would I do,
If it wasn't for –

The somethings I want,
The desires I dream,
The very best of everything?

Swept away,
In the bleakness of this day,
Thick and heavy is the heat,
Gilded by the shade the trees selfishly keep.

Is life worth living if no dreams –
Rush through your heart?
As though a stroke of epiphany's beauty,
Has given you purpose.
Take the day and let your dreams,
Sweep you away to a higher place.

Swept away,
So swept in the depths of the cool night,
The stars, they shine with their wisdom,
As full and as bright.

Yet somehow, I know,
With this desire choking my eyes,
The dreams within my heart,
Shall reveal their lives –

That the brightest star,
All the heavens formed,
Lies in my heart,
Where the desire of love is born.

The Edge of Despair

Anxiety rushes through my head,
A tsunami of thoughts so empty and lifeless,
My mind is starting to feel dead.

Lonely is the pain,
That grasps my heart,
Squeezing it so hard,
The blood rushes through.

No one here to talk to,
No one here to hold me,
No on here to smile at,
No one here but the cold truth.

So I sit here,
And I have absolutely nothing left.
I would be happy,
Because I would trust in God,
If only my faith were that strong.

I will persevere, but I just don't know,
If ever I will not be alone anymore.

Why are some people left in the dark?
They try and they try to push through,
But they always get knocked,
Back into a corner.
No light, endless darkness,
Leads to little belief in happiness.

Is it because those who are supposed,
To care about them,
Are in their own world?
Is it because lonely people,
Do not know how to see the light?

Or is it because they try so hard to love,
And get rejected every time?
I am a lonely person,
Yet I want what everyone else does –

Is it too much to ask to love someone,
That you love,
Even if that person does not know,
That they will love you in the end?

Is it too much to ask,
I gave people a chance,
But in the end – unselfishly,
I want what I want.

It may because I am scared or confused,
Or incredibly lonely that I feel despair,
Nearly pushing me off its edge.

Regardless, I know it's because,
It is taking the shot,
That will make me happy –
Whether or not my shot,
Turns into a goal.

I am on the edge of despair,
Hanging by my fingertips.
I want to let go, maybe,
That will make me happiest,
Because right now,
I am hanging on the edge of despair.

I will only hope for love,
But that does not mean it will come,
No matter how hard I try.
I am standing on the edge of despair.

The edge in which has pushed me so far,
The next tip will throw me off.
Moving on....

Tears

Tears hover over me,
Like shadows in the rain.
I am without an umbrella,
I am without a scarf in the cold light of day.

I shed like a retriever,
I can never shed them all,
For if this world would drown tomorrow,
It would be my heart's fault.

I never breathe because I've learned –
That no breath is a sure thing,
If I take a drag of sweet relief,
Then my life only grows more lifeless.

So, I am now at a dead end,
Picking my poison at every turn,
But I can't seem to pick the taste of my tears,
A venom to take my fears.

So, as I shed these tears,
For everything that life is not,
Everything that life is and could be,
It's because of you I have forgot –

To take a breath for the last time,
Shed one more tear before I die,
Say I love you to all those who made me cry.

Ironically, I will miss these tears,
That made me who I am in Heaven's eyes.

Silhouette

A kiss, an infant lying on your chest,
A bucket of roses spread out,
Along your bed threads,
The shadow of two hearts dancing,
On the chest of a child,
That keeps their lock-et of love alive.
All of these are symbols of love.

Silhouette that shines,
A shadow that is first seen before your eyes,
Then follows you throughout your life,
Protecting you from behind –

When you are old and gray,
When you are down to your last breath,
When you have come to a crossroads,
When you look back at who you are,

What you've done,
And how far you have come,
When you look at your silhouette,
And the shadows
Of life that make it grow,
As things get pushed,
Under the bed,
All gone with life and time,

Do you want to look back at the silhouette –
And see all those you loved,
And all those that loved you?
Will love be in your silhouette,

To make you feel warm –
When all the things, times,
And people you love,
In some way may be gone?

But silhouettes can be cold,
Shadows behind you like ghosts watching,
Your every move.
You can't shake the feeling,
Of regret and sin and hate,
They can make you feel so alone,
In this world of deep sadness.

What if your silhouette,
Didn't shine under the sun?
But instead hid in the darkness,
Growing colder each day,

Because of the choices you once made?
Would you look back and regret,
Not having someone in Heaven,
To greet you when you get there?

Love is like soaring in a sky so beautiful,
With the colors of the moon,
And the sunset and sunrise combined.
Love is like a flying eagle,
A soul soaring into Heaven!

Love is knowing that somehow,
The darkness of the shadows,
That make the silhouette are not all bad –
Like sleeping under the stars,

Or looking at a night cloud,
And seeing the reflection,
Of a head up and lips smiling.

Looking up to Heaven,
Knowing that the shadows always clear,
In the basking glow of dark from light.

So when you look back,
At the end of your life,
And at the silhouette,
That will be staring back at you,
Will you look back and smile –
With a feeling of fulfillment?

Or will you look back,
With a cold-stoned heart and cry?
Will your silhouette reflect,
A ray of sun or the glow of the moon?
Will it stay there lingering –
Like a guilty conscience of a troubled mind?

Will it feel warm and tender –
Like a mama clasping her child in her arms?
Will it feel cold; hard like a gravestone –
That no one ever visits?

The silhouette will know whether or not,
Your future will hold Heaven or Hell.
Still the choice of love is yours.
Don't wait until *now* is over –

For darkness and light clashing together,
Make epic beauty of the soul's silhouette.
They reflect not your age,
But the years lived.

If you remember nothing as time furthers,
Your road and your way,
Remember this one thing,
And it will show you the love,
Still to be given and taken in this life,
Of change, it's truly never too late –

A silhouette can always shine in the dark.

Loneliness Discovered

I discovered loneliness yesterday,
There it was lying in front of me,
Lingering all around me.
Creating a cloud that surrounded me –
Until I could see nothing but the
Blankness of my empty heart.

Like being in an airplane,
As you look out the window,
You can't see the ground,
You used to walk on,
You used to take comfort on,
You used to feel invincible on.

All I can do is discover,
This yearning burning inside,
Loneliness is an empty feeling,
But it's mine in my heart,
To conquer in time.

Shadows of Juliet

Love, right before my eyes,
I am the girl who is uncertain,
To an envisaged life.
To be the girl who makes the heart of man,
Burn like fire on the water –
Shadows of Juliet.

There is a Romeo, for every girl,
Who longs for something more,
A Juliet for every boy,
Who seeks life on the golden shore.
I know that someday,
The one I may or may not find in *this* life,
Will be waiting for me.

Heart ticking like the eternal father of time,
An endless love served from paradise above -
Shadows from my inner Juliet.

So come to me, my love,
In either form or figure,
Release the passion inside my heart of steel.
Though I may die for this love –
The one and only,
Juliet, unknown, is my gateway to forever.

For it is better to have loved and lost,
Than to never have loved at all.
Shadows of Juliet –
I will answer thy true lover's call!

The Cold War

A thousand days in counting,
Since I fell in love with you.

A world as cold as nature,
A mountain higher than Heaven.

I took the chance and climbed,
Stone by stone of your heart.

The higher, the heavier,
My heart still suffocating.

Moving up is a thousand days easier,
Than moving on,
From one mountain to the next.

Every breath I take, huh,
Leaves me a little more breathless.

You're deep elevated heart,
Is colder than the ice frozen over the ocean.

Like an abyss,
Your heart is dark and hallow.

But in your grasp, I remain,
Tightly you anchor my heart.

Fighting to slash the cord that you tug,
My heart drags a little more,

Than you hold me still,
Until the life drains over this cold war.

Broken dreams spilt,
Like blood from the wound you reopened.

Shielding me is my strength,
Given to me by climbing,
Your cold mountain.

I see nothing, I feel everything,
I fear my deepest regret.

Man never wins a war,
Unless in his heart lies a hallow depth.

Years can never mend,
Love, true and faithful.

I tend to this war with my loving hand,
Shielded by the bitterness you left.

Cold is my heart now,
Yet for you this love is now,
Left unrequited.

We will never end this war,
Until we face the fear of each other's eyes.

For the soul sees no boundaries,
Even when lover's die on opposite sides.

Hiding in the Shadows

Last night your longing called for
Anyone out of the darkness –
Who'd be willing to listen.
No one heard your tears,
As they fell off your soft cheek,
And hit the hard ground –
Like a lightning strike without sound.

Hiding in the shadows –
Is a girl who's afraid,
To feel the light of day.
She doesn't want to be exposed,
And left naked in the rain.
A cross that's bare,
Except with her name engraved,
She is afraid to suffer all over again.

So you keep your face hidden,
From the lurking shadows,
That surround your inner space.
Can't let them in for fear,
They'll take control,
And you'll lose yourself to the fall.

Her past haunts her like a shadow,
Mirroring her every move.
The obsession of her thoughts,
Take control of her –
She can't find any peace...

Love left unloved.

Hiding in the shadows,
Hiding in the thickness of this fog,
Hiding so deep,

Hiding in the shadows, she weeps...

Simply Love

Your eyes shine, just at the right time.
They are my refuge,
In all these lonely nights.

The rain is falling from my emerald eyes,
And down my cheeks,
But one look into your eyes,
They shine so bright –
This darkness within me, subsides.

Walk with me, place me at ease,
I am your baby – to this sweet lullaby.
Funny all this time,
I thought you needed me,

The truth is so ironic, 'cause I'm the one –
Who needs you, all this time, all I had to do,
Was gaze into your eyes,
And simply love you.

The truth was so simple to see,
Yet so hard to understand.
But I saw it when you took my hand and –
Guided me back to *my* belong.

Walk with me around the bend,
Place my hand in yours,
I was alone,

Then you gazed into my eyes,
You simply loved me,
In the nick of life's short time.

Simply love you!

Shadowy Pathway

Small rocks align the pathway,
Stained with blood soaked tears,
From my still breathing heart.
Each step I take I turn the page,
On another lonely day in my life.

The trees, thin and tall,
Separated a few feet apart,
Remind me my dreams are ne'er to far,
Ne'er to close enough.

So, I walk on and all I see –
Is the shadowy pathway before me.
Though I ponder where my decision today –
May lead me tomorrow,

There is something more I long for.
The loneliness that surrounds me,
The shadows rising from the dirt,
And into the air as though they understand,

Each thought that keeps me hidden,
Each day that I am awake,
Each step I take,
To follow my fate,

That someday the fog will clear,
And I will have reached the end,
Of a pathway trodden heavily,
With sins, secrets, and sorrow.

But today I keep my head straight,
My eyes opened,
To the burying silence around me.

Heart that is stronger, wiser,
And yet greener than before,
The shadows that surround me,
May clear one day,

The fog may clear,
The oxygen here is closing in,
Leaving me to wonder,
When this shadowy pathway ends –
Where will life lead me then?

PART 4
A STORY WITHOUT AN END

A Story Without An End

I can't always see your face,
Until I close my eyes,
But I can always feel your touch,
Especially when I am sleeping at night.

I cross the line into my dreams,
And you are there waiting for me.
I want so desperately to hold you,
But then I awaken.

Is it time yet? If not, when?
God, to be with the man I love,
Love that will forget to find an end.

Thick as the darkness of night,
Hallow as the fog at sea,
Greater than eternity brought to him,
More than what he's done for me.

So happy was I,
When I peered into his eyes,
Around him felt a fire,
The passion hasn't died.

His soul is an eagle guiding me,
Out of my dark realms,
Of past and present until I realize,
That one day, someday,
I will return to his heart again.

As his spirit lifts mine,
Every time I think of his face,
I hear his voice, a background noise,
Telling me his love isn't far away.

Think of the beauty,
So above earth's boundaries,
That I felt strong enough to love him.
Even stronger to fall,
Into his sea of excitement.

So he is here all around me,
And yet he's gone far enough away,
That I miss him,
Ever so I continue this life the way,
I was meant to live it.

Now I don't feel alone,
Just sometimes without.
For I have lived and I have loved,
I have scattered the ashes,
Of my broken dreams among the sea.

I have learned the truth of this life,
The truth only my heart can speak,
I know that his vision still calls to me.

Need is a mere thought,
While want is a mere desire,
In the grand scheme of love –
I satisfied them all.

I wait now, to be reunited,
With his ocean that has divided,
The heavens and the earth,

And yet brought them together,
Because he and I are still one –
We will always be.

He is still the one for me,
Cold now is his body,
Warm now is his breath on my lips...

Angels gather round,
Being thy witness to true love –
Walk me down the aisle.

Reaching out far enough is his hand,
He is calling me to come home,
I have kept a promise as I have lived a life,
Under the beauty of his star,
And the shadow of his love,
And the song of his soul.

I can now be among him;
I am reunited with love indescribable,
I am all I ever need to be.

We have kissed and time has told,
We have always loved with royal hearts,
We are together forever...

Finally, our love has reached –
A story without an end.

Despair

This shadow that follows,
Me under the sun,
Reminds me of the cold;
The despair that breathes within.

My soul is weary and my mind tired;
Of anxious thoughts and a haunted heart,
Of love never realized,
Of dreams never fulfilled.

Alone, I am here,
Without the wonders,
That once carried me,
Yet the longing was too deep.

This despair I carry,
Like an angel on my shoulder,
Falls through the cracks,
Of my breaking heart,
Shattering in the hallow depths,
Of this lonely soul.

Darkness covers the ocean,
As velvet blue covers the sky,
Life cries out for more, so much more,
Than this despair that in the balance lies.

So, with this song,
A lonely melody,
I sing in the silent air,
Empty is the quietness,
Noise is this despair.

So when I lay my head,
On the pillow beside my shadow,
I will whisper prayers,
Lest my mind fall asleep,
Into the dreams of this dark night.

Despair comes with reason,
Loneliness lingers without guilt,
My star is hidden behind the shadows,
Of the tears running from my eyes.

I feel nothing of anyone,
I see nothing but the dark before,
I hear nothing but my despair,
Calling me, wanting me to give in more.

Things We Forgot To Say

My friend asked me today,
If I would stay with her when the time came
To take her own life away.

She wanted to cheat death,
Beat God,
Even though in the end she knew –
She'd never win.

'Cause no one really knows,
What happens after you die.
And where you will go,
When you don't see the sun's rays of light.

On this earth we all need one another,
To pass the time we take for granted away,
Until we lose the battle,
With things we forgot to say.

Are we ever meant to find;
A piece of Heaven to let us know –
Where we'll go after all is said and done?

Like a flower in the winter,
Life tears until our souls are bare,
And we see the real creature in the mirror –
The one God sees every day.

Too scary so we ignore,
Too much pain we alone can't take away.
On this earth we all need to be loved,
Really loved.

It's so hard, I know,
To forget after you forgive,
And to leave your hurt unhealed,
To let Him hold you again.

But trust in your heart,
The truth that will never change.
Stop fighting with your lover,
God owes you the same.

In the end when hope is forcing us,
Ever near to his care,
If he knows you truly love him,
He will be there.

And you'll know the truth,
Dear friend,
Of the meaning to your life,
And you'll long for a safe haven,

One you believe can keep you,
From the death of life.
In the end, I know,
That no matter the reason,
I pray to end up in His Heaven,

Then lie naked in a six-foot-deep box,
Somewhere –
With no one to care.

Gentle

It's that gentle smile I see every day,
Like picking out a flower in the pouring rain.
It's not crazy, not coarse,
Just gentle and true.

Those eyes are so real and yet so soft,
They tell me you love me,
They tell me I am your world,
They tell me I am better than just okay.

The softness of your skin,
And the gentleness of your voice,
The beauty unraveling itself in your hair,
As it sways with the wind,
Unafraid and eager,
Yet gentle and strong.

I see myself in you,
Meek and mild,
Cheek and wild.
It's everything I want to be,
Everything my heart longs for –

A gentle ear to listen,
A kind voice that is angelic to the ears,
A soft hand when I just need,
Someone to be there.

Thank you for being real,
For being gentle,
For being...

To me you are love,
Gentle, beautiful, brave, and strong.
Never failing, never holding on,

And never letting go.
Embrace me in your invisible heart,
A gentle love to a gentle smile.

We will always be one,
My beautiful precious,
Gentle child!

Fear of the Shadows

Fear of the shadows,
So deep within you,
The darkness that fogs,
Your heart and soul.

Nothing like the missing beat,
Of the one you love,
To make you feel,
The cold ground beneath.

Nothing like your still beating heart,
To make you wish you couldn't breathe.

Fear of death can make,
Even the strongest of man fall to his knees.
Shadows of the past that never go away,
Like falling rain forming an ocean,
With each shadow your mind goes astray.

Then somehow you wake up,
Cold with sweat drowning your body,
You emerge from the chamber within,
You ignore the shadows' cries.

Shadows of the present moment,
Keep you confused and lonely,
Depression is the emptiness you feel,
When grief of life is eminent.

Shadows of the future call you by name,
Teasing you with empty promises,
Like the man,
That stepped on your heart with his refrain.

Still you wonder more and more,
As your present grows darker,
If the fear that is holding you back,
Is truly because of one fear,
That encompasses,
Surpasses, and overcomes all fears –

The greatest fear of all,
Is the shadow of your own.

Years Within

Life can be seen,
Through the eyes,
Within me lies many years.

I am young enough,
To know nothing,
And desire more.

Yet I am old enough,
To know all I need,
And realize what I have lost.

Ever mindful of the wisdom,
Deeper the truth,
Clearer and clearer is thy yearning's call.

Finding myself within,
The nightmares I cannot live without,
Dreams are dreams and nothing more.

Still I awaken to their call,
And try my best to overcome this loneliness,
Years within have given me the strength –
To carry on.

Love Never Dies

I loved you, for a day.
In this life it seems as though,
That is all we have.

So I loved you, for a lifetime.
It was the time when ours was rare,
Like a dying breed of life somewhere.

Now you are gone, it doesn't matter how far.
Cause if you are not by my side,
Then so far away you truly are.

Love never dies, some people believe.
It is like a flower,
It grows old and it withers,
But the roots planted once before, simmer.

Simmer, nearly like an eternal flame.
Yet, today, I realize,
That the flower blooms no more,
You are not waiting outside my window,
Nor my door.

I wonder, why that flower has gone.
Maybe the soil is so thick,
That suffocation has sucked the life,
Out of that one little seed.

Like a tick on the skin,
Life is drained from each of us,
As time goes on,
Until life is no more.

Still the eternal sunshine awaits...
Breathing out light and life,
Like a child ascending,
From thy mother's womb.

Somehow that tiny seed,
Catches fire again....
Maybe it will grow,
If life is meant to live from thy soul.

I will be waiting for love,
A true love,
A love that *never* dies.

Shadows of Thyself

Shadows peer through the window,
Their reflection forms a face.
The face is bold and scary,
The face is the girl within I never knew.

Till I learned that life was for,
Not the faint or meek at heart.
Life is for the bold and the scary,
Life is for those who find a worth of living.

I look into the shadows,
Peer through to the other side,
Where I see myself in Heaven,
Calling me to leave this lonely life.

Am I afraid of death?
Afraid of the gathering shadows around?
No, I guess I'd say I'm afraid of life.
For knowing this life,

Is the scariest thing,
My heart could ever long for.
For beauty lies within,
The depths of thyself and thy soul,

Yet fear covers this soul,
Shadows sucked into a bottle,
My ship is stuck in the one place,
It never thought it'd remain,

Shadows port to Heaven's call,
In thyself the soul's refrain.
Like a blanket over fire,
Shadows suffocate this life of mine.

My spirit is now homesick,
For a place where my heart,
Can live freely through eternal time.
So I look into these shadows,

And comprehend the scariest light of all,
Yet the most beautiful tarry,
Is the one the shadows call.
I look into these shadows,

And I see so many things,
My past has spiraled,
Into my emotional emptiness,
My present has brought me back,
To harsh reality again,

My future is a shadow
I seek the days through.
Yet I pray that my dreams,
Which are ever true,

Will make my time of this life,
Worth something.
Without my voice, I am nothing,
Without my heart, I am dark.

Without my spirit's soul willing to rise,
To the northern sky and endless horizon,
I will never know the sweet longing,
Of Heaven's flow.

I look upon the shadows,
I stare into the depths of the dark,
I search for nothing because I know,
I am peering into my soul,

The shadows gather close,
I realize I am looking again,
At the shadows of my lonely soul,
These are the shadows of thyself.

Shadows...

Nightmare's Reach

Reaching into the deepest depths,
Within my soul,
Reaching out to capture,
My trembling body,
Reaching farther and farther,
To pull me into Hell's fire.
I just can't take this anymore.

I am walking around in a circle,
Around the demons that encompass me,
Fire and brimstone,
Cracks between my skin's thick surface,
Screams break deafening silence,
I am so hot, I don't think I can survive.

Demons of despair shadow my every move,
Reaching into my nightmares until at night,
My heart doesn't rest but rather lies still,

Waiting for the flashbacks,
Shadows of the past,
Visions of the unknown future,
Fears of the present moment,
To be over.

When will reality's nightmare be over?

Shadows of Love

Shadows of love harbor my regret,
For ignoring the call of my instincts,
To take the chance on happiness.

Shadows that linger inside my lonely mind,
Are those of so many lovers I left behind.

True love comes but in many forms,
Yet so rare it is for us to recognize,
Like a foreigner,
We only choose to travel,
Love's road once.

For love is so much harder than hate,
The effort we place into it,
Isn't always received the same.

But to give love, no matter the reason,
The person, the time,
Is using the gift of each infant heart born,
Under these transforming skies.

Love is the boundary,
Between Heaven and Hell,
It is the life within us,
It gives us a reason to trust,
The heart within ourselves.

Still so many things,
Love has stolen without warning,
Haunt me as I follow the shadows.

The sun reveals the secrets of the night,
Love has taught me heartache is more,
Than just a time sensitive emotion,

It is a being that can overwhelm us,
Break our spirits and weary our souls,
Beg Love for mercy,
This I have come to know.

Still I believe the one thing,
That can see through the mists of tears,
Conquer the fears we can't seem to let go,
And achieve so much more,
Than we ever thought possible –

Is Love –
Sweet, hard, and true,
It is the invisible shadow,
That makes us fight,
Another day, another night,
Another war to win the light.

Love, thought of as meek,
Love thought of as a fallback for the weak,
Love thought of as unworthy to live for,

Is the strongest being ever,
We are blessed enough to come face to face,
Free will is sometimes the shunning,
That keeps Love away.

But what do we rely on when –
The storm takes ne'er all our life away,
We rely on Love to help us,
When we can't find the strength,
Within ourselves,
To pick up and move on.

Shadows of Love,
Reflecting all around us,
Like rays from the full moon,
Playing with us through the windows,
Peering into our souls,
Piercing through our hearts.

Reflection of the ones loved,
The ones lost,
And the ones that remain in our shadows.
Love quenches the thirst for knowing,
Love is the eternal being,
Evermore we have a way to live on.

Shadows are memories,
That make us believe fear,
Is Love's greatest enemy,
Like God to the Devil.

Gather 'round us until Love answers,
Our call for more,
Than we could ever ask for.

So, even though, so many times,
Love has let me down,
I still choose to give it another chance.

Because it's not the love from the outside,
To which I look upon,
It is the Love within thyself,
That gives me the strength,
To conquer my enemy mirage.

Tragedy of Us

What's it like to touch heaven?
What's it like to live among the stars?
What's it like to watch this world from afar?

What's it like hear the voice of an angel,
When it's standing by your ear?
Or to have wings that match the colors,
Only your heart can bring?

Do you ever see my future –
Revealed before your eyes?
If you do, is your wish to tell me?
Or do you like to pick out the mask,
In which my future is disguised?

Do you feel as bad as I do –
When, in a quiet moment,
The memory of us,
Digs deeper than the love,
In Heaven could ever be?

Or is pain obsolete?
Is pain an unfeeling deity,
Whom can't touch your heart?
Your heart deserves no pain,
That's why God chose you first.
Still I can't help but hope,
That my pain is matched,
By the love we can no longer share.

For even in time – if we are ever to reunite,
The time, the forces of the universe,
Make us spend apart –
Is time lost in the hallow galaxy.
This world is colder now,
Raided of the time that could have been.
Yet somehow, I know my deed –
To carry on...

And if I must do *time* without you,
Then I must make the best,
So to honor our promise.

To leave this world,
Colder than when I came in,
Is to be without you.
To leave this world,
Colder than when I was born unto,
Is a tragedy.
The only tragedy worse,
Than losing you.
The tragedy of us.

What is it like to see all and feel good?
What is it like to live,
In the heart of angel's wood?
What is it like to be where,
Forever never dies?
What is like to know eternal beauty,
In Love's eyes?

What is it like to touch God?

Cast Away the Shadows

Cast away the shadows,
Open your tired eyes,
So the light may pierce into your soul,
And tears, may the warmth of the sun dry.

Throw the curtains to the sides,
Reveal yourself to the heavens,
Feel your spirit resurrect your life.

Heaven will call your shadows,
Like ghosts in the night they will appear,
And find their way to the other side,
Where loves waits to heal the memories,
Of your fears.

So, cast away the shadows,
Breathe in Mother's Nature's air,
Feel the tingling awaken you,
Focus on the dream that keeps you here.

Never give up for the fight is yours to win,
Love is always on your side,
As long as your heart is willing to give in,
To the light of darkness,
Cast away the shadows.

Each day is a step closer to Heaven,
Each dream is a goal waiting to be conquered,
And each shadow is comfort,
To give your heart rest,
From life's relentless weariness.

Take comfort in the shadows,
That lead and followed you here,
They are reminders of the crosses,
The strength you've earned from bare.

Cast away the fears within,
Your effervescent soul,
Leave the emptiness at the door,
Let love live and life carry on.

Finding yourself in the memories of the past,
Awakening to the dawn of a new day,
And starry night,
Dreaming of an epic future,
Your journey begins when your spirit,
Is ready to take flight.

The call of the wild echoing through –
The confines of the invisible heart,
Seek the peace they have waited for,
Let your love be your light in the dark.

Cast away the shadows,
Conquer all your fears,
Let your love shine through you,
A courage to keep ever near you...

Cast away your shadows!

PART 5
THE AUTHOR'S REFLECTION

Shadows – Michelle Sarasin

Mystery of the Shadows

Mystery of the Shadows...

Lying on my pillow,
Hair draped over the edge,
Like legs dangling off the pier,
Each strand has a place here.

The heart ponders the reason for night,
Darkness remains,
Because I am blinded by the light,
My eyes pine for the glow of knowing,
The meaning of the mystery of the shadows.

Life has called me,
To yearn for more rest,
With each passing day.
Still I wonder when I awake,
Will I understand the –

Mystery of the Shadows...

Mystery of the Shadows...

Mystery of the Shadows...

Shadows – Michelle Sarasin

Author's Reflection

Shadows within my own life continue to remain a mystery. Each one has meaning whether it is linked to the past, present or future. After reading each poem, I hope that in some small way it gave you an understanding of how complex the human soul truly is.

I wanted to write an author's reflection so that things you may not have understood when initially reading the collection can now come to a clearer and brighter light. Each poem was written from deep personal experiences that continue to haunt me and yet, somehow, teach me more about the human condition.

Every person is different from another, no matter how equal we all truly are. Every soul has their own story and every heart has their own longing. I wanted my personal experiences to bring forth an understanding of how intricate the human spirit really is.

I hope that in some way you felt connected, healed, inspired, or simply entertained and comforted by these poems. The darkness is something that humans have been told to fear – but I've learned it is truly something that we should embrace like an enemy turned friend.

No matter what I write about; every story, every poem, every song, and every detail will be interpreted differently as this book is passed from writer to reader and so forth. The spirit of the book, *Shadows*, which has a metaphorical way of connecting us to a more spiritual and soulful self, is what will connect us together no matter how different our stories and our lives are.

I cannot say this book will be of any help to you, fellow poetry reader. But I can tell you that if ever you feel you face the darkness of life or even the brighter times fearfully, feel free to pick up this poetry collection again and reintroduce yourself to a deeper side within that you never knew existed.

Ultimately, *Shadows*, is the reflection of one woman's heart and life. It is my feelings and thoughts and experiences, that has led to this collection of poems. I hope that you enjoyed it as much I did when writing it over the years. Through this journey, I have been able to heal, in very small ways, a part of me that I cannot share by word of mouth.

To share this collection of poems, has truly been a gift and I thank you for reading *Shadows*!

Love,
Michelle Sarasin
Author/Poetess of *Shadows*

About the Author

Michelle Sarasin is a writer, actress, and singer-songwriter from New England. Her work in both writing and music has been called "a beautiful emotional experience" one that continues to inspire people around the world.

Shadows, her first collection of poems released publicly, is one of many collections to come under the publisher M.N. Sulwyn Books.

For more info on the author/singer please visit
michellesarasin.com
and
Like *Michelle Sarasin Official* on Facebook!

Other Titles from M.N. Sulwyn Books

The Intimate You: 200 *Writing Prompts to Help Your Heart Reflect and Heal*

Dreams Within You: 200 *Writing Prompts to Discover the Power Within*